Keynes, the Man

Keynes, the Man

Murray N. Rothbard

LvMI
MISES INSTITUTE

Ludwig von Mises Institute
518 West Magnolia Avenue
Auburn, Alabama 36832
www.mises.org

ISBN: 978-1-933550-72-5

The General Theory was not truly revolutionary at all but merely old and oft-refuted mercantilist and inflationist fallacies dressed up in shiny new garb, replete with newly constructed and largely incomprehensible jargon.

Murray N. Rothbard

Contents

Keynes, the Man

JOHN MAYNARD KEYNES, the man—his character, his writings, and his actions throughout life—was composed of three guiding and interacting elements. The first was his overweening egotism, which assured him that he could handle all intellectual problems quickly and accurately and led him to scorn any general principles that might curb his unbridled ego. The second was his strong sense that he was born into, and destined to be a leader of, Great Britain's ruling elite.

Both of these traits led Keynes to deal with people as well as nations from a self-perceived position of power and dominance. The third element was his deep hatred and contempt for the values and virtues of the bourgeoisie, for conventional morality, for savings and thrift, and for the basic institutions of family life.

Originally published in *Dissent on Keynes: A Critical Appraisal of Keynesian Economics*, edited by Mark Skousen. New York: Praeger (1992), pp. 171–98.

Born to the Purple

KEYNES was born under special circumstances, an heir to the ruling circles not only of Britain but of the British economics profession as well. His father, John Neville Keynes, was a close friend and former student of Alfred Marshall, Cambridge professor and unchallenged lion of British economics for half a century. Neville Keynes had disappointed Marshall by failing to live up to his early scholarly promise, producing only a bland treatise on the methodology of economics, a subject disdained as profoundly "un-English" (J. N. Keynes [1891] 1955).

The classic refuge for a failed academic has long been university administration, and so Neville happily buried himself in the controllership and other powerful positions in Cambridge University administration. Marshall's psyche compelled him to feel a moral obligation toward Neville that went beyond the pure loyalty of friendship, and that sense of obligation was carried over to Neville's beloved son Maynard. Consequently, when Maynard eventually decided to pursue a career as an economist at Cambridge, two extremely powerful figures at that university—his father and Alfred Marshall—were more than ready to lend him a helping hand.

The Cambridge Apostle

THE MOST favored education available to the English elite was secured for Maynard by his doting father. First, he was a scholarship student at "College" in Eton, the intellectual subdivision of England's most influential public school. From there, Maynard went on to King's College, which, along with Trinity, was one of the two dominant colleges at Cambridge University.

At King's, Maynard was soon tapped for coveted membership in the secret society of the Apostles, an organization that rapidly shaped his values and his life. Keynes grew to social and intellectual maturity within the confines of this small, incestuous world of secrecy and superiority. The Apostles were not simply a social club, in the manner of Ivy League secret fraternities. They were also a self-consciously intellectual elite, especially interested in philosophy and its applications to aesthetics and life.

Apostle members were chosen almost exclusively from King's and Trinity, and they met every Saturday evening behind locked doors to deliver and discuss papers.[1] During the rest of the week, members virtually lived in each others' rooms. Moreover, Apostleship was not simply an undergraduate affair; it was membership for life and cherished as such. For the rest of their lives, adult Apostles (known as "Angels"), including Keynes, would often return to

[1] Asking himself why the eminent constitutional historian Frederic W. Maitland had no influence over the Apostles in this era, even though a member, Derek Crabtree answers that Maitland was unfortunate enough to hold his chair at Downing College, one of the lesser, uninfluential colleges at Cambridge (see Crabtree 1980, pp. 18–19).

Cambridge for meetings, and they participated actively in recruiting new undergraduates.

In February 1903, at the age of 20, John Maynard Keynes took his place as Apostle number 243 in a chain that stretched back to the society's founding in 1820. For the next five or six formative years, Maynard spent almost all his private life among the Apostles, and his values and attitudes were shaped accordingly. Furthermore, most of his adult life was spent among older and newer Apostles, their friends, or their relations.

An important reason for the potent effect of the Society of the Apostles on its members was its heady atmosphere of secrecy. As Keynes's biographer, Robert Skidelsky, writes,

> One should never underestimate the effect of secrecy. Much of what made the rest of the world seem alien sprang from this simple fuel. Secrecy was a bond which greatly amplified the Society's life relative to its members' other interests. It is much easier, after all, to spend one's time with people from whom one does not have to keep large secrets; and spending much time with them reinforces whatever it was that first drew them together. (Skidelsky 1983, p. 118; see also Deacon 1986)

The extraordinary arrogance of the Apostles is best summed up in the Society's Kantian half joke: that the Society alone is "real," whereas the rest of the world is only "phenomenal." Maynard himself would refer to non-Apostles as "phenomena." What all this meant was that the world outside was regarded as less substantial, less worthy of attention than the Society's own collective life.

It was a joke with a serious twist (Skidelsky 1983, p. 118). "It was owing to the existence of the Society," wrote Apostle Bertrand Russell in his *Autobiography,* "that I soon got to know the people best worth knowing." Indeed, Russell remarked that when the adult Keynes left Cambridge, he traveled the world with a feeling of being the bishop of a sect in foreign parts. "True salvation for Keynes," remarked Russell perceptively, "was elsewhere, among the faithful at Cambridge" (Crabtree and Thirlwall 1980, p. 102).

Or, as Maynard himself wrote during his undergraduate days in a letter to his friend and co-leader, Giles Lytton Strachey, "Is it monomania—this colossal moral superiority that we feel? I get the feeling that most of the rest [of the world outside the Apostles] never see anything at all—too stupid or too wicked" (Skidelsky 1983, p. 118).[2]

Two basic attitudes dominated this hermetic group under the aegis of Keynes and Strachey. The first was their overriding belief in the importance of personal love and friendship, while scorning any general rules or principles that might limit their own egos; and the second, their animosity toward and contempt for middle-class values and morality. The Apostolic confrontation with bourgeois values included praise for avant-garde aesthetics, holding homosexuality to be morally superior (with bisexuality a distant second[3]), and hatred for such traditional family values as thrift or any emphasis on the future or long run, as compared to the present. ("In the long run," as Keynes would later intone in his famous phrase, "we are all dead.")

---

[2] When the philosopher John E. McTaggart, a lecturer at Trinity who had been an Apostle since the 1880s, got married late in life, he assured the Apostles that his wife was merely "phenomenal" (Skidelsky 1983, p. 118).

[3] Bertrand Russell, who was a decade older than Keynes, did not like the Keynes/Strachey group that dominated undergraduate members during the first decade of the 20th century, largely because of their conviction that homosexuality was morally superior to heterosexuality.

Bloomsbury

AFTER graduation from Cambridge, Keynes and many of his Apostle colleagues took up lodgings in Bloomsbury, an unfashionable section of north London. There they formed the now-famous Bloomsbury Group, the center of aesthetic and moral avant-gardism that constituted the most influential cultural and intellectual force in England during the 1910s and 1920s.

The formation of the Bloomsbury Group was inspired by the death of that eminent Victorian philosopher and classical liberal, Sir Leslie Stephen, in 1904. The young Stephen children, who felt liberated by the departure of their father's stern moral presence, promptly set up house in Bloomsbury and began to hold Thursday evening salons. Thoby Stephen, while not an Apostle, was a close friend at Trinity of Lytton Strachey. Strachey and other Apostles, as well as another of Strachey's good friends from Trinity, Clive Bell, became regular salon guests.

After Thoby died in 1906, Vanessa Stephen married Bell, and Bloomsbury gatherings divided into two groups. Since Clive was a budding art critic and Vanessa a painter, they established the Friday Club salons, concentrating on the visual arts. Meanwhile, Virginia and Adrian Stephen resumed the Thursday emphases on literature, philosophy, and culture. Eventually, Trinity Apostle Leonard Woolf, a friend and contemporary of Keynes, married Virginia Stephen. In late 1909, Keynes moved to a Bloomsbury house very close to the Stephens', sharing a flat there with Bloomsbury artist Duncan Grant, a cousin of Strachey's.

Bloomsbury's values and attitudes were similar to those of the Cambridge Apostles, albeit with more of an artistic twist. With a major emphasis on rebellion against Victorian values, it is no wonder that Maynard Keynes was a distinguished Bloomsbury member. One particular emphasis was pursuit of avant-garde and formalistic art—pushed by art critic and Cambridge Apostle Roger Fry, who later returned to Cambridge as Professor of Art. Virginia Stephen Woolf would become a prominent exponent of formalistic fiction. And all of them energetically pursued a lifestyle of promiscuous bisexuality, as was brought to light in Michael Holroyd's (1967) biography of Strachey.

As members of the Cambridge cultural coterie, the Bloomsbury Group enjoyed inherited, although modest, wealth. But, as time went on, most of the financing for the various Bloomsbury exhibits and projects came from their loyal member Maynard Keynes. As Skidelsky writes, Keynes "came to give Bloomsbury financial muscle, not just by making a great deal of money himself [largely through investment and financial speculation], which he spent lavishly on Bloomsbury causes, but by his ability to organize financial backing for their enterprises." Indeed, from the first World War onwards it was almost impossible to find any enterprise, cultural or domestic, in which members of Bloomsbury were involved, which did not benefit in some way from his largesse, his financial acumen, or his contacts. (1983, p. 250; see also pp. 242–51).

The Moorite Philosopher

THE GREATEST impact on Keynes's life and values, the great conversion experience for him, came not in economics but in philosophy. A few months after Keynes's initiation into the Apostles, G.E. Moore, a professor of philosophy at Trinity who had become an Apostle a decade earlier than Keynes, published his magnum opus, *Principia Ethica* (1903). Both at the time and in reminiscence three decades later, Keynes attested to the enormous impact that the *Principia* had had upon him and his fellow Apostles.

In a letter at the time of its publication, he wrote that the book "is a stupendous and entrancing work, *the greatest* on the subject" [Keynes's italics], and a few years later he wrote to Strachey, "It is *impossible* to exaggerate the wonder and *originality* of Moore. … How amazing to think that only we know the rudiments of a true theory of ethic[s]." And, in a 1938 paper to the Bloomsbury Group, entitled "My Early Beliefs," Keynes recalls that the *Principia's* "effect on *us*, and the talk which preceded and followed it, dominated and perhaps still dominates, everything else." He added that the book "was exciting, exhilarating, the beginning of a new renaissance, the opening of a new heaven on earth" (Skidelsky 1983, pp. 133–34; Keynes [1951] 1972, pp. 436–49). Very strong words about a book on technical philosophy!

What is their source? First was the personal charisma that Moore exercised upon the students at Cambridge. But beyond that personal magnetism, Keynes and his friends were attracted not so much to Moore's doctrine itself as to the particular interpretation and twist that they themselves gave to that doctrine. Despite their enthusiasm, Keynes and his friends accepted only what they held to be Moore's *personal* ethics (i.e., what they called Moore's "religion"), while they totally rejected his *social* ethics (i.e., what they called his "morals").

Keynes and his fellow Apostles enthusiastically embraced the idea of a "religion" composed of moments of "passionate contemplation and communion" of and with objects of love or friendship. They repudiated, however, all social morals or general rules of conduct, totally rejecting Moore's penultimate chapter on "Ethics in Relation to Conduct." As Keynes states in his 1938 paper,

> In our opinion, one of the greatest advantages of his [Moore's] religion was that it made morals unnecessary. … We entirely repudiated a personal liability on us to obey general rules. We claimed the right to judge every individual case on its merits, and the wisdom to do so successfully. This was a very important part of our faith, violently and aggressively held, and for the outer world it was our most obvious and dangerous characteristic. We repudiated entirely customary morals, conventions and traditional wisdom. We were, that is to say, in the strict sense of the term, immoralists. (Keynes [1951] 1972, pp. 142–43)

Shrewd contemporary observers perceptively summed up the attitude of Keynes and his fellow Apostles. Bertrand Russell wrote that Keynes and Strachey twisted Moore's teachings; they "aimed at a life of retirement among fine shades and nice feelings, and conceived of the good as consisting in the passionate mutual admirations of a clique of the elite" (Welch 1986, p. 43). Or, as Beatrice Webb neatly observed, Moorism among the Apostles was "nothing but a metaphysical justification for doing what you like—and what other people disapprove of" (ibid.).

The question then arises, how seriously did this immoralism, this rejection of general rules that would restrict one's ego, mark Keynes's adult life? Sir Roy Harrod, a disciple and hagiographical biographer, insists that immoralism, as with any other unpleasant aspect of Keynes's personality, was only an adolescent phase, quickly outgrown by his hero.

But many other aspects of his career and thought confirm Keynes's lifelong immoralism and disdain for the bourgeoisie. Moreover, in his 1938 paper, delivered at the age of 55, Keynes confirmed his continuing adherence to his early views, stating that immoralism is "still my religion under the surface. … I remain and always will remain an immoralist" (Harrod 1951, pp. 76–81; Skidelsky 1983, pp. 145–46; Welch 1986, p. 43).

In a notable contribution, Skidelsky demonstrates that Keynes's first important scholarly book, *A Treatise on Probability* (1921), was not unrelated to the rest of his concerns. It grew out of his attempt to copper rivet his rejection of Moore's proposed general rules of morality. The beginnings of the *Treatise* came in a paper, which Keynes read to the Apostles in January 1904, on Moore's spurned chapter, "Ethics in Relation to Conduct." Refuting Moore on probability occupied Keynes's scholarly thoughts from the beginning of 1904 until 1914, when the manuscript of the *Treatise* was completed.

He concluded that Moore was able to impose general rules upon concrete actions by employing an empirical or "frequentist" theory of probability, that is, through observation of empirical frequencies we could have certain knowledge of the probabilities of *classes* of events. To destroy any possibility of applying general rules to particular cases, Keynes's *Treatise* championed the classical a priori theory of probability, where probability fractions are deduced purely by logic and have nothing to do with empirical reality. Skidelsky makes the point well:

> Keynes's argument, then, can be interpreted as an attempt to free the individual to pursue the good … by means of egotistic actions, since he is not required to have certain knowledge of the probable consequences of his actions in order to act rationally. It is part, in other words, of his continuing campaign against Christian morality. This would have been appreciated

> by his audience, although the connection is not obvious to the modern reader. More generally, Keynes links rationality to expediency. The circumstances of an action become the most important consideration in judgments of probable rightness. … By limiting the possibility of certain knowledge Keynes increased the scope for intuitive judgment. (Skidelsky 1983, 153–54)

We cannot get into the intricacies of probability theory here. Suffice it to say that Keynes's a priori theory was demolished by Richard von Mises (1951) in his 1920s work, *Probability, Statistics, and Truth*. Mises demonstrated that the probability fraction can be meaningfully used only when it embodies an empirically derived law of entities which are homogeneous, random, and indefinitely repeatable.

This means, of course, that probability theory can only be applied to events which, in human life, are confined to those like the lottery or the roulette wheel. (For a comparison of Keynes and Richard von Mises, see D.A. Gillies [1973, pp. 1–34].) Incidentally, Richard von Mises's probability theory was adopted by his brother Ludwig, although they agreed on little else (L. von Mises [1949] 1966, pp. 106–15).

The Burkean Political Theorist

"IF MOORE was Keynes's ethical hero, Burke may lay strong claim to be being his political hero," writes Skidelsky (1983, p. 154). Edmund Burke? What could that conservative worshiper of tradition have in common with Keynes, the statist and rationalist central planner? Once again, as with Moore, Keynes venerated his man with a Keynesian twist, selecting the elements that fitted his own character and temperament.

What Keynes took from Burke is revealing. (Keynes presented his views in a lengthy, undergraduate, prize-winning English essay on "The Political Doctrines of Edmund Burke.") There is, first, Burke's militant opposition to general principles in politics and, in particular, his championing of expediency against abstract natural rights. Secondly, Keynes agreed strongly with Burke's high time preference, his downgrading of the uncertain future versus the existing present. Keynes therefore agreed with Burke's conservatism in the sense that he was hostile to "introducing present evils for the sake of future benefits."

There is also the right-wing expression of Keynes's general deprecation of the long run, when "we are all dead." As Keynes put it, "It is the paramount duty of governments and of politicians to secure the wellbeing of the community under the case in the present, and not to run risks overmuch for the future" (ibid., pp. 155–56).

Thirdly, Keynes admired Burke's appreciation of the "organic" ruling elite of Great Britain. There were differences over policy, of course, but Keynes joined Burke in hailing the system of aristocratic rule as sound, so long as governing personnel were chosen from the existing organic elite. Writing of Burke, Keynes noted, "the machine itself [the British state] he held to be sound enough if only the ability and integrity of those in charge of it could be assured" (ibid., p. 156).

In addition to his neo-Burkean disregard for principle, lack of concern for the future, and admiration for the existing British ruling class, Keynes was also sure that devotion to truth was merely a matter of taste, with little or no place in polities. He wrote: "A preference for truth or for sincerity *as a method* may be prejudice based on some aesthetic or personal standard, inconsistent, in politics, with practical good" (Johnson 1978, p. 24).

Indeed Keynes displayed a positive taste for lying in politics. He habitually made up statistics to suit his political proposals, and he would agitate for world monetary inflation with exaggerated hyperbole while maintaining that "words ought to be a little wild—the assault of thoughts upon the unthinking." But, revealingly enough, once he achieved power, Keynes admitted that such hyperbole would have to be dropped: "When the seats of power and authority have been attained, there should be no more poetic license" (Johnson and Johnson 1978, pp. 19–21).

The Economist: Arrogance and Pseudo Originality

MAYNARD Keynes's approach in economics was not unlike his attitude in philosophy and life in general. "I am afraid of 'principle,'" he told a Parliamentary committee in 1930 (Moggridge 1969, p. 90). Principles would only restrict his ability to seize the opportunity of the moment and would hamper his will to power. Hence, he was eager to desert his earlier beliefs and change his mind on a dime, depending on the situation.

His stand on free trade serves as a blatant example. As a good Marshallian, his one, seemingly fixed, lifelong politicoeconomic principle was a devoted adherence to freedom of trade. At Cambridge he wrote to a good friend, "Sir, I hate all priests and protectionists. … Down with pontiffs and tariffs." For the next three decades, his political interventions were almost solely concerned with championing free trade (Skidelsky 1983, pp. 122, 227–29).

Then, suddenly, in the spring of 1931, Keynes loudly called for protectionism, and during the 1930s, he led the parade for economic nationalism and for policies frankly designed to "beggar-thy-neighbor." But during World War II, Keynes swung back to free trade. Never did any soul-searching or even hesitation seem to hobble his lightning-fast changes.

Indeed, in the early 1930s, Keynes was widely ridiculed in the British press for his chameleon views. As Elizabeth Johnson writes, He was Keynes the India-rubber man: the *Daily News and Chronicle* of 16 March 1931, carried an article headed, "Economic Acrobatics of Mr. Keynes"—and illustrated it by a sketch of "A Remarkable Performance. Mr. John Maynard Keynes as the 'boneless man,' turns his back on himself and swallows a draught" (1978, p. 17).

Keynes, however, did not trouble himself about charges of inconsistency, considering himself always right. It was particularly easy for Keynes to adopt this conviction since he cared not a tap for principle. He was therefore always ready to change horses in pursuit of expanding his ego through political power.

As time went on, Elizabeth Johnson writes, Keynes "had a clear idea of his role in the world; he was … the chief economic adviser to the world, to the Chancellor of the Exchequer of the day, to the French minister of finance, … to the president of the United States." Pursuit of power for himself and a ruling class meant, of course, increasing adherence to the ideas and institutions of a centrally managed economy.

Among the good men of the organic elite governing the nation, he placed himself in the crucial role of scholar-technician, the 20th century version of the "philosopher-king" or, at least, the philosopher guiding the king. It is no wonder that Keynes "hailed President [Franklin D.] Roosevelt as the first head of state to take theoretical advice as the basis for large-scale action" (Johnson and Johnson 1978, pp. 17–18).

Action is what Keynes sought from government, especially with Keynes himself making the plans and calling the shots. As Johnson writes,

> His opportunism meant that he reacted to events immediately and directly. He would produce an answer, write a memorandum, publish at once, whatever the issue. … In the World War II Treasury, he nearly drove some of his colleagues crazy with his propensity to keep a finger in every pie. "Don't just stand there, do something" would have been his present-day motto (ibid., p. 19).

Johnson notes that Keynes's

> instinctive attitude to any new situation was to assume, first, that nobody was doing anything about it, and, secondly, that if they were, they were doing it wrong. It was a lifetime habit of mind based on the conviction that he was armed with superior brains ... and, Cambridge Apostle that he was, gilled with superior sensibilities. (Ibid., p. 33)

One striking illustration of Maynard Keynes's unjustified arrogance and intellectual irresponsibility was his reaction to Ludwig von Mises's brilliant and pioneering *Treatise on Money and Credit,* published in German in 1912. Keynes had recently been made the editor of Britain's leading scholarly economic periodical, Cambridge University's *Economic Journal.* He reviewed Mises's book, giving it short shrift. The book, he wrote condescendingly, had "considerable merit" and was "enlightened," and its author was definitely "widely read," but Keynes expressed his disappointment that the book was neither "constructive" nor "original" (Keynes 1914). This brusque reaction managed to kill any interest in Mises's book in Great Britain, and *Money and Credit* remained untranslated for two fateful decades.

The peculiar point about Keynes's review is that Mises's book was highly constructive and systematic, as well as remarkably original. How could Keynes not have seen that? This puzzle was cleared up a decade and a half later, when, in a footnote to his own *Treatise on Money,* Keynes impishly admitted that "in German, I can only clearly understand what I already know—so that new ideas are apt to be veiled from me by the difficulties of the language" (Keynes 1930a: I, p. 199 n.2). Such unmitigated gall. This was Keynes to the hilt: to review a book in a language where he was incapable of grasping new ideas, and then to attack that book for not containing anything new, is the height of arrogance and irresponsibility.[4]

---

[4] In view of his friendship with Keynes, Hayek's account of this episode characteristically misses Keynes's arrogance and gall, treating the story as if it were merely unfortunate

Another aspect of Keynes's swaggering conceit was his conviction that much of what he did was original and revolutionary. His letter to G.B. Shaw in 1935 is well known:

> I believe myself to be writing a book on economic theory that will largely revolutionise … the way the world thinks about economic problems. … For myself I don't merely hope what I say, in my own mind I'm quite sure. (Hession 1984, p. 279)

But this belief in his braggadocio was not confined to *The General Theory*.

Bernard Corry points out that "From about the beginning of his economic work he claimed to be revolutionising the subject." So imbued was Keynes with faith in his own creativity that he even proclaimed great originality in a paper on business cycles that was based on D.H. Robertson's *Study of Industrial Fluctuations*, shortly after the book was published in 1913. Corry links this attitude to the insistent emphasis of the Bloomsbury Group on "originality" (by which, of course, they mainly meant their own). Originality, he points out, was "one of the fixations of the Bloomsbury Group" (Crabtree and Thirlwall 1980, pp. 96–97; Corry 1986, pp. 214–15, 1978, pp. 3–34).

Keynes was greatly aided in his claims of originality by the tradition of economics that Alfred Marshall had managed to establish at Cambridge. As a student of Marshall and a young Cambridge lecturer under Marshall's aegis, Keynes easily absorbed the Marshallian tradition.

It was not that Marshall himself claimed blazing originality, although he did make claims to independent inventions of marginal utility and he was secretive, jealous of students who might steal his ideas. Marshall developed the strategy of maintaining a hermetically sealed Marshallian world at Cambridge (and hence in

---

that Keynes did not know German better: "The world might have been saved much suffering if Lord Keynes's German had been a little better" (Hayek [1956] 1984, pp. 219; see also Rothbard 1988, pp. 28).

British economics generally). He created the myth that in his 1890 magnum opus, the *Principles of Economics*, he had constructed a higher synthesis, incorporating the valid aspects of all previously competing and clashing theories (deductivism and inductivism, theory and history, marginal utility and real cost, short run and long run, Ricardo and Jevons).[5]

Because he successfully pushed this myth, he therefore spawned the universal view that "it's all in Marshall," that, after all, there was no need to read anyone else. For if Marshall had harmonized all the one-sided, one-eyed economic views, there was no longer any reason except antiquarianism to bother to read them. As a result, the modal Cambridge economist read only Marshall, spinning out and elaborating on cryptic sentences or passages in the Great Book. Marshall himself spent the rest of his life reworking and elaborating The Text, publishing no less than eight editions of the *Principles* by 1920.

For the rest, there was the legendary Cambridge "oral tradition," in which Marshall's students and disciples were delighted to listen to and pass on the "Great Man's" words, as well as to read his lesser seminal writings in manuscript or in commission hearings, for Marshall kept most of his shorter writings out of publication until near the end of his life. Thus, the Cambridge Marshallians could take unto themselves the aura of a priestly caste, the only ones privy to the mysteries of the sacred writings denied to lesser men.

The tightly sealed world of Marshallian Cambridge soon dominated Great Britain; there were few challengers in that country. This dominance was accelerated by the unique role of Cambridge and Oxford in British social and intellectual life, especially in the years before the educational explosion that followed World War II. Since the days of Adam Smith, David Ricardo, and J.S. Mill, Great Britain

---

[5] There is no space here to elaborate my conviction that this was a false and even pernicious myth, that what Marshall really did was not to synthesize but to reestablish the dominance of Ricardo and Mill and their long-run equilibrium and cost-of-production theories, overlaying them with a thin veneer of trivialized marginal-utility analysis.

had managed to dominate economic theory throughout the world, so Marshall and his sect managed to assume hegemony not only of Cambridge economics but of the world (see Crabtree 1980, pp. 101–05).[6]

---

[6] Thus, as late as World War II and shortly thereafter, my honors seminar at Columbia College consisted of a chapter-by-chapter reading and analysis of Marshall's Principles. And when I was preparing for my doctoral oral examination in the history of thought, the venerable John Maurice Clark told me that there was no real need for me to read Jevons because "all his contributions are in Marshall."

"The Swindler"

THE YOUNG Keynes displayed no interest whatsoever in economics; his dominant interest was philosophy. In fact, he completed an undergraduate degree at Cambridge without taking a single economics course. Not only did he never take a degree in the subject, but the only economics course Keynes ever took was a single-term graduate course under Alfred Marshall.

He found that spell of economics exciting, however, as it appealed both to his theoretical interests and to his thirst for cutting a giant swath through the real world of action. In the fall of 1905, he wrote to Strachey, "I find economics increasingly satisfactory, and I think I am rather good at it. I want to manage a railroad or organise a Trust or at least swindle the investing public" (Harrod 1951, p. 111).[7]

Keynes, in fact, had recently embarked on his lifelong career as investor and speculator. Yet Harrod was constrained to deny vigorously that Keynes had begun speculating before 1919.

Asserting that Keynes had "no capital" before then, Harrod explained the reason for his insistence in a book review six years after the publication of his biography: "It is important that this should be clearly understood, since there were many ill-wishers … who asserted that he took advantage of inside information when in the Treasury (1915–June 1919) in order to carry out successful

---

[7] As Skidelsky points out, it is typical of Roy Harrod's whitewashing biography that, in quoting this letter, he leaves out his hero's remark about "swindling the investing public" (Skidelsky 1983, pp. 165n).

speculations" (Harrod 1957). In a letter to Clive Bell, author of the book under review and an old Bloomsburyite and friend of Keynes, Harrod pressed the point further: "The point is important because of the beastly stories, which are very widespread ... about his having made money dishonourably by taking advantage of his Treasury position" (ibid.; cf. Skidelsky 1983, pp. 286–88).

Despite Harrod's insistence to the contrary, however, Keynes had indeed set up his own "special fund" and had begun to make investments by July 1905. By 1914, Keynes was speculating heavily in the stock market and, by 1920, had accumulated £16,000, which would amount to about $200,000 at today's prices. Half of his investment was made with borrowed money.

It is not clear at this point whether his fund was used for investment or for more speculative purposes, but we do know that his capital had increased by more than threefold. Whether Keynes used inside Treasury information to make such investment decisions is still unproven, although suspicions certainly remain (Skidelsky 1983, pp. 286–88).

Even if we cannot prove the charge of swindling against Keynes, we must consider his behavior in the light of his own bitter condemnation of financial markets as "gambling casinos" in *The General Theory*. It seems probable, therefore, that Keynes *believed* his successes at financial speculation to have swindled the public, although there is no reason to think he would have regretted that fact. He did realize, however, that his father would disapprove of his activity.[8]

[8] In a letter to his mother on September 3, 1919. Keynes wrote of his speculation in foreign exchange, "which will shock father but out of which I hope to do very well" (Harrod 1951, pp. 288). For a penetrating critique of Keynes's views on speculation as gambling, see Hazlitt ([1959] 1973, pp. 179–85).

Keynes and India

WHILE at Eton, young Keynes (aged 17 and 18) witnessed a wave of anti-imperialist sentiment in the wake of Britain's war against the Boers in South Africa. Yet he was never influenced by that sentiment. As Skidelsky notes,

> Throughout his life he assumed the Empire as a fact of life and never showed the slightest interest in discarding it. … He never much deviated from the view that, all things being considered, it was better to have Englishmen running the world than foreigners. (Skidelsky 1983, p. 91)

In late 1905, despite Marshall's importuning, Keynes abandoned graduate studies in economics after one term and, the following year, took Civil Service exams, gaining a clerkship in the India Office. In the spring of 1907, Keynes was transferred from the Military Department to the Revenue, Statistics, and Commerce Department. While he was to become an expert on Indian affairs, he nevertheless blithely assumed that British rule was not to be questioned: Britain simply disseminated good government in places which could not develop it on their own.

"Maynard," Skidelsky points out, "always saw the Raj from Whitehall; he never considered the human and moral implications of imperial rule or whether the British were exploiting the Indians." In the grand imperialist tradition of the Mills and Thomas Macaulay in 19th-century England, moreover, Keynes never felt the need to travel to India, to learn Indian languages, or to read any books on the area except as they dealt with finance (ibid., p. 176).

Despite his rise to high levels of the Civil Service, Keynes soon grew tired of his quasi sinecure and tried to return to Cambridge by way of a teaching post. Finally, in the spring of 1908, Marshall wrote to Keynes, offering him a lectureship in economics. Although Marshall was on the point of retirement, he easily persuaded his friend, favorite student, and handpicked successor, Arthur C. Pigou, to follow Marshall's practice of paying for the lectureship out of his own salary; Neville Keynes promptly offered to match the stipend.

In 1908, Keynes happily took up the insular role of lecturing in Marshallian economics at his old school, King's College, Cambridge. But most of his time and energy were spent as a busy man of affairs in London (Corry 1978, p. 5). One of his functions was to be an informal but valued adviser to the India Office; indeed, his association with the office actually expanded after 1908 (Keynes 1971, p. 17). As a result, he played an important role in Indian monetary affairs, writing his first major journal article on India for the *Economic Journal* in 1909; writing influential memoranda out of which grew his first book, the brief monograph on *Indian Currency and Finance* in 1913; and playing an influential role on the Royal Commission on Indian Finance and Currency, to which distinguished post he was appointed before the age of 30.

Keynes's role in Indian finance was not only important but also ultimately pernicious, presaging his later role in international finance. Upon converting India from a silver to a gold standard in 1892, the British government had stumbled into a gold-exchange standard, instead of the full gold-coin standard that had marked Britain and the other major Western nations. Gold was not minted as coin or otherwise available in India, and Indian gold reserves for rupees were kept as sterling balances in London rather than in gold per se.

To most government officials, this arrangement was only a halfway measure toward an eventual full gold standard; but Keynes hailed the new gold-exchange standard as progressive, scientific, and moving toward an ideal currency. Echoing centuries-old inflationist views, he opined that gold coin "wastes" resources, which can be "economized" by paper and foreign exchange.

The crucial point, however, is that a phony gold standard, as a gold-exchange standard must be, allows far more room for monetary management and inflation by central governments. It takes away the public's power over money and places that power in the hands of the government. Keynes praised the Indian standard as allowing a far greater "elasticity" (a code word for monetary inflation) of money in response to demand. Moreover, he specifically hailed the report of a US government commission in 1903 advocating a gold-exchange standard in China and other Third World silver countries—a drive by progressive economists and politicians to bring such nations into a US dominated and managed gold-dollar bloc (Keynes 1971, pp. 60–85; see also Parrini and Sklar 1983; Rosenberg 1985).

Indeed, Keynes explicitly looked forward to the time when the gold standard would disappear altogether, to be replaced by a more "scientific" system based on a few key national paper currencies. "A preference for a tangible reserve currency," Keynes opined, is "a relic of a time when governments were less trustworthy in these matters than they are now" (1971, p. 51). Here was the foreshadowing of Keynes's famous dismissal of gold as a "barbarous relic." More broadly, Keynes's early monetary views presaged the disastrous gold-exchange standard engineered by Britain during the 1920s, as well as the deeply flawed Bretton Woods scheme of a managed gold-dollar imposed by the United States—with the help of Britain and Lord Keynes—at the end of World War II.

The Cambridge economist, however, was not content to defend the gold-exchange status quo in India. Believing that the march toward managed inflation was not proceeding rapidly enough, he urged the creation of a central bank (or "State Bank") for India, thus enabling centralization of reserves, far greater monetary elasticity, and far more monetary expansion and inflation. Although he was unable to convince the Royal Commission to come out in support of a central bank, he was highly influential in its final report.

The report included his central-bank view in an appendix, and Keynes also led the harsh cross-examination of pro-gold coin standard and anti-central bank witnesses. An interesting footnote to the affair was the reaction to Keynes's central-bank appendix by his old teacher, Alfred Marshall. Marshall wrote Keynes that he was "entranced by it as a prodigy of constructive work" (ibid., p. 268).

Keynes generally liked to tackle economic theory in order to solve practical problems. His primary motivation for plunging into the Indian currency question was to defend the record of his first and most important political patron, Edwin Samuel Montagu, of the influential Montagu and Samuel families of London international banking. Montagu had been president of the Cambridge Union, the university debating society, when Keynes was an undergraduate, and Keynes had become a favorite of his. In the 1906 general elections, Keynes had campaigned for Montagu's successful bid for a Parliamentary seat as a Liberal.

In late 1912, when Montagu was Undersecretary of State for India, a scandal developed in Indian finance. The Indian government, of which Montagu was second-in-command, had contracted secretly with the banking firm of Samuel Montagu and Company to purchase silver. It turned out that nepotism had figured strongly in this contract. Lord Swaythling, a senior partner in the firm, was the father of undersecretary Edwin S. Montagu; another partner, Sir Stuart Samuel, was the brother of Herbert Samuel, postmaster general of the Asquith government (see Skidelsky 1983, p. 273).

Selling the General Theory

KEYNES'S *General Theory* was, at least in the short run, one of the most dazzlingly successful books of all time. In a few short years, his "revolutionary" theory had conquered the economics profession and soon had transformed public policy, while old-fashioned economics was swept, unhonored and unsung, into the dustbin of history.

How was this deed accomplished? Keynes and his followers would answer, of course, that the profession simply accepted a starkly self-evident truth. And yet *The General Theory* was not truly revolutionary at all but merely old and oft-refuted mercantilist and inflationist fallacies dressed up in shiny new garb, replete with newly constructed and largely incomprehensible jargon. How, then, the swift success?

Part of the reason, as Schumpeter has pointed out, is that governments as well as the intellectual climate of the 1930s were ripe for such conversion. Governments are always seeking new sources of revenue and new ways to spend money, often with no little desperation; yet economic science, for over a century, had sourly warned against inflation and deficit spending, even in times of recession.

Economists—whom Keynes was to lump into one category and sneeringly disparage as "classical' in *The General Theory*—were the grouches at the picnic, throwing a damper of gloom over attempts by governments to increase their spending. Now along came Keynes, with his modern "scientific" economics, saying that the old "classical" economists had it all wrong: that, on the contrary, it was the government's moral and scientific duty to spend, spend, and spend; to incur deficit upon deficit, in order to save the economy from such vices as thrift and balanced budgets and unfettered capitalism; and to generate recovery from the depression. How welcome Keynesian economics was to the governments of the world!

In addition, intellectuals throughout the world were becoming convinced that laissez-faire capitalism could not work and that it was responsible for the Great Depression. Communism, fascism, and various forms of socialism and controlled economy became popular for that reason during the 1930s. Keynesianism was perfectly suited to this intellectual climate.

But there were also strong internal reasons for the success of *The General Theory*. By dressing up his new theory in impenetrable jargon, Keynes created an atmosphere in which *only* brave young economists could possibly understand the new science; no economist over the age of thirty could grasp the New Economics. Older economists, who, understandably, had no patience for the new complexities, tended to dismiss *The General Theory* as nonsense and refused to tackle the formidably incomprehensible work. On the other hand, young economists and graduate students, socialistically inclined, seized on the new opportunities and bent themselves to the rewarding task of figuring out what *The General Theory* was all about.[9]

---

[9] Harry Johnson put the strategy perceptively: "In this process, it helps greatly to give old concepts new and confusing names. … [T]he new theory had to have the appropriate degree of difficulty to understand. This is a complex problem in the design of new theories. The new theory had to be so difficult to understand that senior academic colleagues would find it neither easy nor worthwhile to study, so that they would waste their efforts on peripheral theoretical issues, and so offer themselves as easy market for criticism and dismissal by their younger and hungrier colleagues. At the same time, the new theory had to appear both difficult enough to challenge the intellectual interest of young colleagues and students, but actually easy enough for them to master adequately with a sufficient investment of intellectual endeavor. These objectives Keynes's General Theory managed to achieve: it neatly shelves the old and established scholars, like Pigou and Robertson, enabled the most enterprising middle-and lower-middle-aged like Hansen, Hicks, and Joan Robinson to jump on and drive the bandwagon, and permitted a whole generation of students … to escape from the slow and soul-destroying process

Paul Samuelson has written of the joy of being under 30 when *The General Theory* was published in 1936, exulting, with Wordsworth, "Bliss was it in that dawn to be alive, but to be young was very heaven." Yet this same Samuelson who enthusiastically accepted the new revelation also admitted that *The General Theory*

> is a badly written book; poorly organized. ... It abounds in mares' nests of confusions. ... I think I am giving away no secrets when I solemnly aver—upon the basis of vivid personal recollection—that no one else in Cambridge, Massachusetts, really knew what it was all about for some twelve to eighteen months after publication. (Samuelson [1946] 1948, p. 145; Hodge 1986, pp. 21–22)

It must be remembered that the now-familiar Keynesian cross, IS-LM diagrams, and the system of equations were not available to those trying desperately to understand *The General Theory* when the book was published; indeed, it took 10 to 15 years of countless hours of manpower to figure out the Keynesian system. Often, as in the case of both Ricardo and Keynes, the more obscure the content, the more successful the book, as younger scholars flock to it, becoming acolytes.

Also important to the success of *The General Theory* was the fact that, just as a major war creates a large number of generals, so did the Keynesian revolution and its rude thrusting aside of the older generation of economists create a greater number of openings for younger Keynesians in both the profession and the government.

Another crucial factor in the sudden and overwhelming success of *The General Theory* was its origin in the most insular university of the most dominant economic national center in the

---

of acquiring wisdom by osmosis from their elders and the literature into an intellectual realm in which youthful iconoclasm could quickly earn its just reward (in its own eyes at least) by the demolition of the intellectual pretensions of its academic seniors and predecessors. Economics, delightfully, could be reconstructed from scratch on the basis of a little Keynesian understanding and a lofty contempt for the existing literature—and so it was" (1978, pp. 188–89).

world. For a century and a half, Great Britain had arrogated to itself the role of dominance in economics, with Smith, Ricardo, and Mill all aggrandizing this tradition. We have seen how Marshall established his dominance at Cambridge and that the economics he developed was essentially a return to the classical Ricardo/Mill tradition.

As a prominent Cambridge economist and student of Marshall, Keynes had an important advantage in furthering the success of the ideas in *The General Theory*. It is safe to say that if Keynes had been an obscure economics teacher at a small, Midwestern American college, his work, in the unlikely event that it even found a publisher, would have been totally ignored.

In those days before World War II, Britain, not the United States, was the most prestigious world center for economic thought. While Austrian economics had flourished in the United States before World War I (in the works of David Green, Frank A. Fetter, and Herbert J. Davenport), the 1920s to early 1930s was largely a barren period for economic theory. Antitheoretical institutionalists dominated American economics during this period, leaving a vacuum that was easy for Keynes to fill.

Also important to his success was Keynes's tremendous stature as an intellectual and politicoeconomic leader in Britain, including his prominent role as a participant in, and then severe critic of, the Versailles treaty. As a Bloomsbury member, he was also important in British cultural and artistic circles.

Moreover, we must realize that in pre-World War II days only a small minority in each country went to college and that the number of universities was both small and geographically concentrated in Great Britain. As a result, there were very few British economists or economics teachers, and they all knew each other. This created considerable room for personality and charisma to help convert the profession to Keynesian doctrine,

The importance of such external factors as personal charisma, politics, and career opportunism was particularly strong among the disciples of F.A. Hayek at the London School of Economics. During the early 1930s, Hayek at the LSE and Keynes at Cambridge were the polar antipodes in British economics, with Hayek converting many of Britain's leading young economists to Austrian (that is, Misesian) monetary, capital, and business-cycle theory.

Additionally, Hayek, in a series of articles, had brilliantly demolished Keynes's earlier work, his two-volume *Treatise on Money*, and many of the fallacies Hayek exposed applied equally well to *The General Theory* (see Hayek 1931a, 1931b, 1932). For Hayek's students and followers, then, it must be said that they knew better. In the realm of theory, they had already been inoculated against *The General Theory*. And yet, by the end of the 1930s, every one of Hayek's followers had jumped on the Keynesian bandwagon, including Lionel Robbins, John R. Hicks, Abba P. Lerner, Nicholas Kaldor, G.L.S. Shackle, and Kenneth E. Boulding.

Perhaps the most astonishing conversion was that of Lionel Robbins. Not only had Robbins been a convert to Misesian methodology as well as to monetary and business-cycle theory, but he had also been a diehard pro-Austrian activist. A convert since his attendance at the Mises *privatseminar* in Vienna in the 1920s, Robbins, highly influential in the economics department at LSE, had succeeded in bringing Hayek to LSE in 1931 and in translating and publishing Hayek's and Mises's works.

Despite being a longtime critic of Keynesian doctrine before *The General Theory*, Robbins's conversion to Keynesianism was apparently solidified when he served as Keynes's colleague in wartime economic planning. There is in Robbins's diary a decided note of ecstatic rapture that perhaps accounts for his astonishing abasement in repudiating his Misesian work, *The Great Depression* (1934).

Robbins's repudiation was published in his 1971 *Autobiography*: "I shall always regard this aspect of my dispute with Keynes as the greatest mistake of my professional career, and the book, *The Great Depression*, which I subsequently wrote, partly in justification of this attitude, as something which I would willingly see forgotten" (Robbins 1971, p. 154). Robbins's diary entries on Keynes during World War II can only be considered an absurdly rapturous personal view. Here is Robbins at a June 1944 pre–Bretton Woods draft conference in Atlantic City:

> Keynes was in his most lucid and persuasive mood: and the effect was irresistible… . Keynes must be one of the most remarkable men that have ever lived—the quick logic, the wide vision, above all the incomparable sense of the fitness of words, all combine to make something several degrees beyond the limit of ordinary human achievement. (Ibid., p. 193)

Only Churchill, Robbins goes on to say, is of comparable stature. But Keynes is greater, for he

> uses the classical style of our life and language, it is true, but it is shot through with something which is not traditional, a unique unearthly quality of which one can only say that it's pure genius. The Americans sat entranced as the godlike visitor sang and the golden light played all around. (Ibid., pp. 208–12 cf. Hession 1984, p. 342)

This sort of fawning can only mean that Keynes possessed some sort of strong personal magnetism to which Robbins was susceptible.[10]

Central to Keynes's strategy in putting *The General Theory* over were two claims: first, that he was revolutionizing economic theory, and second, that he was the first economist—aside from a few "underworld" characters, such as Silvio Gesell—to concentrate on the problem of unemployment. All previous economists, whom he lumped together as "classical," he said, assumed full employment

---

[10] Robbin's biographer, D.P. O'Brien, labors hard to maintain that, despite what he admits is Robbins's "elaborate" and "exaggerated contrition," Robbins never really, deep down, converted to Keynesianism. But O'Brien is unconvincing, even after he tries to show how Robbins waffled on some issues. Moreover, O'Brien admits that Robbins dropped his Misesian macro approach, and he fails to mention Robbins's astonishing treatment of Keynes as "godlike" (O'Brien 1988, pp. 14–16, 117–20).

and insisted that money was but a "veil" for real processes and was therefore not a truly disturbing presence in the economy.

One of Keynes's most unfortunate effects was his misconceiving of the history of economic thought, since his devoted legion of followers accepted Keynes's faulty views in *The General Theory* as the last word on the subject. Some of Keynes's highly influential errors may be attributed to ignorance, since he was little trained in the subject and mostly read work by his fellow Cantabrigians. For example, in his grossly distorted summary of Say's law ("supply creates its own demand"), he sets up a straw man and proceeds to demolish it with ease (1936, p. 18).

This erroneous and misleading restatement of Say's law was subsequently repeated (without quoting Say or any of the other champions of the law) by Joseph Schumpeter, Mark Blaug, Axel Leijonhufvud, Thomas Sowell, and others. A better formulation of the law is that the supply of one good *constitutes* demand for one or more other goods (see Hutt 1974, p. 3).

But ignorance cannot account for Keynes's claim that he was the first economist to try to explain unemployment or to transcend the assumption that money is a mere veil exerting no important influence on the business cycle or the economy. Here we must ascribe to Keynes a deliberate campaign of mendacity and deception—what would now be called euphemistically "disinformation."

Keynes knew all too well of the existence of the Austrian and LSE Schools, which had flourished in London as early as the 1920s and more obviously since 1931. He himself had personally debated Hayek, the chief Austrian at LSE, in the pages of *Economica*, the LSE journal. The Austrians in London attributed continuing large-scale unemployment to wage rates kept above the free-market wage by combining union and government action (e.g., in extraordinarily generous unemployment-insurance payments).

Recessions and business cycles were ascribed to bank credit and monetary expansion, as fueled by the central bank, which pushed interest rates below genuine time-preference levels and created overinvestment in higher-order capital goods. These then had to be liquidated by a recession, which in turn would emerge as soon as the credit expansion stopped. Even if he had not agreed with this analysis, it was unconscionable for Keynes to ignore the very existence of this school of thought then prominent in Great Britain, a school which could never be construed as ignoring the impact of monetary expansion on the real state of the economy.

In order to conquer the world of economics with his new theory, it was critical for Keynes to destroy his rivals within Cambridge itself. In his mind, he who controlled Cambridge controlled the world. His most dangerous rival was Marshall's handpicked successor and Keynes's former teacher, Arthur C. Pigou. Keynes began his systematic campaign of destruction against Pigou when Pigou rejected his previous approach in the *Treatise on Money*, at which point Keynes also broke with his former student and close friend, Dennis H. Robertson, for refusing to join the lineup against Pigou.

The most glaring misstatement in *The General Theory*, and one which his disciples accepted without question, is the outrageous presentation of Pigou's views on money and unemployment in Keynes's identification of Pigou as the major contemporary "classical" economist who allegedly believed that there is always full employment and that money is merely a veil causing no disruptions in the economy—this about a man who wrote *Industrial Fluctuations* in 1927 and *Theory of Unemployment* in 1933, which discuss at length the problem of unemployment! Moreover, in the latter book, Pigou explicitly repudiates the money veil theory and stresses the crucial centrality of money in economic activity.

Thus, Keynes lambasted Pigou for allegedly holding the "conviction … that money makes no real difference except frictionally and that the theory of unemployment can be worked out … as being based on 'real' exchanges." An entire appendix to chapter 19 of *The General Theory* is devoted to an assault on Pigou, including the claim that he wrote only in terms of real exchanges and real wages, not money wages, and that he assumed only flexible wage rates (Keynes 1936, pp. 19–20, pp. 272–79).

But, as Andrew Rutten notes, Pigou conducted a "real" analysis only in the first part of his book; in the second part, he not only brought money in, but pointed out that any abstraction from money distorts the analysis and that money is crucial to any analysis of the exchange system. Money, he says, cannot be abstracted away and cannot act in a neutral manner, so "the task of the present part must be to determine in what way the monetary factor causes the average amount of, and the fluctuation in, employment to be different from what they otherwise would have been."

Therefore, added Pigou, "it is illegitimate to abstract money away [and] leave everything else the same. The abstraction proposed is of the same type that would be involved in thinking away oxygen from the earth and supposing that human life continues to exist" (Pigou 1933, pp. 185, 212). Pigou extensively analyzed the interaction of monetary expansion and interest rates along with changes in expectations, and he explicitly discussed the problem of money wages and "sticky" prices and wages.

Thus, it is clear that Keynes seriously misrepresented Pigou's position and that this misrepresentation was deliberate, since, if Keynes read any economists carefully, he certainly read such prominent Cantabrigians as Pigou. Yet, as Rutten writes, "These conclusions should not come as a surprise, since there is plenty of evidence that Keynes and his followers misrepresented their predecessors" (Rutten 1989, p. 14). The fact that Keynes engaged in this systematic deception and that his followers continue to repeat the fairy tale about Pigou's blind "classicism" shows that there is a deeper reason for the popularity of this legend in Keynesian circles. As Rutten writes,

> There is one plausible explanation for the repetition of the story of Keynes and the classics. … This is that the standard account is popular because it offers simultaneously an explanation of, and a justification for, Keynes's success: without the

> General Theory, we would still be in the economic dark ages. In other words, the story of Keynes and the Classics is evidence for the General Theory. Indeed, its use suggests that it may be the most compelling evidence available. In this case, proof that Pigou did not hold the position attributed to him is … evidence against Keynes. … [This conclusion] raises the … serious question of the methodological status of a theory that relies so heavily on falsified evidence. (Ibid., p. 15)

In his review of *The General Theory*, Pigou was properly scornful of Keynes's "macédoine of misrepresentations," and yet such was the power of the tide of opinion (or of the charisma of Keynes) that, by 1950, after Keynes's death, Pigou had engaged in the sort of abject recantation indulged in by Lionel Robbins, which Keynes had long tried to wrest from him (Pigou 1950; Johnson and Johnson 1978, p. 179; Corry 1978, p. 11–12).

But Keynes used tactics in the selling of *The General Theory* other than reliance on his charisma and on systematic deception. He curried favor with his students by praising them extravagantly, and he set them deliberately against non- Keynesians on the Cambridge faculty by ridiculing his colleagues in front of these students and by encouraging them to harass his faculty colleagues. For example, Keynes incited his students with particular viciousness against Dennis Robertson, his former close friend.

As Keynes knew all too well, Robertson was painfully and extraordinarily shy, even to the point of communicating with his faithful, longtime secretary, whose office was next to his own, only by written memoranda. Robertson's lectures were completely written out in advance, and because of his shyness he refused to answer any questions or engage in any discussion with either his students or his colleagues. And so it was a particularly diabolic torture for Keynes's radical disciples, led by Joan Robinson and Richard Kahn, to have baited and taunted Robertson, harassing him with spiteful questions and challenging him to debate (Johnson and Johnson 1978, pp. 136ff.).

Keynes's Political Economy

IN *The General Theory*, Keynes set forth a unique politico-economic sociology, dividing the population of each country into several rigidly separated economic classes, each with its own behavioral laws and characteristics, each carrying its own implicit moral evaluation. First, there is the mass of consumers: dumb, robotic, their behavior fixed and totally determined by external forces. In Keynes's assertion, the main force is a rigid proportion of their total income, namely, their determined "consumption function."

Second, there is a subset of consumers, an eternal problem for mankind: the insufferably bourgeois savers, those who practice the solid puritan virtues of thrift and farsightedness, those whom Keynes, the would-be aristocrat, despised all of his life. All previous economists, certainly including Keynes's forbears Smith, Ricardo, and Marshall, had lauded thrifty savers as building up long-term capital and therefore as responsible for enormous long-term improvements in consumers' standard of living. But Keynes, in a feat of prestidigitation, severed the evident link between savings and investment, claiming instead that the two are unrelated.

In fact, he wrote, savings are a drag on the system; they "leak out" of the spending stream, thereby causing recession and unemployment. Hence Keynes, like Mandeville in the early 18th century, was able to condemn thrift and savings; he had finally gotten his revenge on the bourgeoisie.

By also severing interest returns from the price of time or from the real economy and by making it only a monetary phenomenon, Keynes was able to advocate, as a linchpin of his basic political program, the "euthanasia of the rentier" class: that is, the state's expanding the quantity of money enough so as to drive down the rate of interest to zero, thereby at last wiping out the hated creditors. It should be noted that Keynes did not want to wipe out investment: on the contrary, he maintained that savings and investment were separate phenomena. Thus, he could advocate driving down the rate of the interest to zero as a means of maximizing investment while minimizing (if not eradicating) savings.

Since he claimed that interest was purely a monetary phenomenon, Keynes could then also sever the existence of an interest rate from the scarcity of capital. Indeed, he believed that capital is not *really* scarce at all. Thus, Keynes stated that his preferred society "would mean the euthanasia of the rentier, and consequently, the euthanasia of the cumulative oppressive power of the capitalist to exploit the scarcity-value of capital."

But capital is not *really* scarce: "Interest today rewards no genuine sacrifice, any more than does the rent of land. The owner of capital can obtain interest because capital is scarce, just as the owner of land can obtain rent because land is scarce. But whilst there may be intrinsic reasons for the scarcity of land, there are no intrinsic reasons for the scarcity of capital." Therefore, "we might aim in practice … at an increase in the volume of capital until it ceases to be scarce, so that the functionless investor [the rentier] will no longer receive a bonus." Keynes made it clear that he looked forward to a gradual annihilation of the "functionless" rentier, rather than to any sort of sudden upheaval (Keynes 1936, pp. 375–76; see also Hazlitt [1959] 1973, pp. 379–84).[11]

Keynes then came to the third economic class, to whom he was somewhat better disposed: the investors. In contrast to the passive

[11] See also the illuminating article by Andrew Rutten (1989). I am indebted to Dr. Rutten for calling this article to my attention.

and robotic consumers, investors are *not* determined by an external mathematical function. On the contrary, they are brimful of free will and active dynamism. They are also not an evil drag on the economic machinery, as are the savers. They are important contributors to everyone's welfare.

But, alas, there is a hitch. Even though dynamic and full of free will, investors are erratic creatures of their own moods and whims. They are, in short, productive but irrational. They are driven by psychological moods and "animal spirits." When investors are feeling their oats and their animal spirits are high, they invest heavily, but too much; overly optimistic, they spend too much and bring about inflation. But Keynes, especially in *The General Theory*, was not really interested in inflation; he was concerned about unemployment and recession, caused, in his starkly superficial view, by pessimistic moods, loss of animal spirits, and hence underinvestment.

The capitalist system is, accordingly, in a state of inherent macroinstability. Perhaps the market economy does well enough on the micro-, supply-and-demand level. But in the macro world, it is afloat with no rudder; there is no internal mechanism to keep its aggregate spending from being either too low or too high, hence causing recession and unemployment or inflation.

Interestingly enough, Keynes came to this interpretation of the business cycle as a good Marshallian. Ricardo and his followers of the Currency School correctly believed that business cycles are generated by expansions and contractions of bank credit and the money supply, as generated by a central bank, whereas their opponents in the Banking School believed that expansions of bank money and credit were merely passive effects of booms and busts and that the real cause of business cycles was fluctuation in business speculation and expectations of profit—an explanation very close to Pigou's later theory of psychological mood swings and to Keynes's focus on animal spirits.

John Stuart Mill had been a faithful Ricardian except in this one crucial area. Following his father, Mill had adopted the Banking

School's causal theory of business cycles, which was then adopted by Marshall (Trescott 1987; Perlman 1989, pp. 88–89).

To develop a way out, Keynes presented a fourth class of society. Unlike the robotic and ignorant consumers, this group is described as full of free will, activism, and knowledge of economic affairs. And unlike the hapless investors, they are not irrational folk, subject to mood swings and animal spirits; on the contrary, they are supremely rational as well as knowledgeable, able to plan best for society in the present as well as in the future.

This class, this deus ex machina external to the market, is of course the state apparatus, as headed by its natural ruling elite and guided by the modern, scientific version of Platonic philosopher kings. In short, government leaders, guided firmly and wisely by Keynesian economists and social scientists (naturally headed by the great man himself), would save the day. In the politics and sociology of *The General Theory*, all the threads of Keynes's life and thought are neatly tied up.

And so the state, led by its Keynesian mentors, is to run the economy, to control the consumers by adjusting taxes and lowering the rate of interest toward zero, and, in particular, to engage in "a somewhat comprehensive socialisation of investment." Keynes contended that this would not mean total state Socialism, pointing out that

> it is not the ownership of the instruments of production which it is important for the State to assume. If the State is able to determine the aggregate amount of resources devoted to augmenting the instruments and the basic rate of reward to those who own them, it will have accomplished all that is necessary. (Keynes 1936, p. 378)

Yes, let the state control investment completely, its amount and rate of return in addition to the rate of interest; then Keynes would allow private individuals to retain formal ownership so that, within the overall matrix of state control and dominion, they could still retain "a wide field for the exercise of private initiative and responsibility." As Hazlitt puts it,

> Investment is a key decision in the operation of any economic system. And government investment is a form of socialism. Only confusion of thought, or deliberate duplicity, would deny this. For socialism, as any dictionary would tell the Keynesians, means the ownership and control of the means of production by government. Under the system proposed by Keynes, the government would *control* all investment in the means of production and would *own* the part it had itself directly invested. It is at best mere muddleheadedness, therefore, to present the Keynesian nostrums as a free enterprise or "individualistic" *alternative to* socialism. (Hazlitt [1959] 1973, p. 388; cf. Brunner 1987, pp. 30, 38)

There was a system that had become prominent and fashionable in Europe during the 1920s and 1930s that was precisely marked by this desired Keynesian feature: private *ownership*, subject to comprehensive government *control* and planning. This was, of course, fascism.

Where did Keynes stand on overt fascism? From the scattered information now available, it should come as no surprise that Keynes was an enthusiastic advocate of the "enterprising spirit" of Sir Oswald Mosley, the founder and leader of British fascism, in calling for a comprehensive "national economic plan" in late 1930. By 1933, Virginia Woolf was writing to a close friend that she feared Keynes was in the process of converting her to "a form of fascism." In the same year, in calling for national self-sufficiency through state control, Keynes opined that "Mussolini, perhaps, is acquiring wisdom teeth" (Keynes 1930b, 1933, p. 766; Johnson and Johnson 1978, p. 22; on the relationship between Keynes and Mosley, see Skidelsky 1975, pp. 241, 305–6; Mosley 1968, pp. 178, 207, 237–38, 253; Cross 1963, pp. 35–36).

But the most convincing evidence of Keynes's strong fascist bent was the special foreword he prepared for the German edition of *The General Theory*. This German translation, published in late

1936, included a special introduction for the benefit of Keynes's German readers and for the Nazi regime under which it was published. Not surprisingly, Harrod's idolatrous *Life* of Keynes makes no mention of this introduction, although it was included two decades later in volume seven of the *Collected Writings* along with forewords to the Japanese and French editions.

The German introduction, which has scarcely received the benefit of extensive commentary by Keynesian exegetes, includes the following statements by Keynes:

> Nevertheless the theory of output as a whole, which is what the following book purports to provide, is much more easily adapted to the conditions of a totalitarian state, than is the theory of production and distribution of a given output produced under conditions of free competition and a lance measure of laissez-faire. (Keynes 1973 [1936], p. xxvi. Cf. Martin 1971, pp. 200–5; Hazlitt [1959] 1973, p. 277; Brunner 1987, pp. 38ff.)

As for communism, Keynes was less enthusiastic. On the one hand, he admired the young, intellectual, English Communists of the late 1930s because they reminded him, oddly enough, of the "typical nonconformist English gentlemen who ... made the Reformation, fought the Great Rebellion, won us our civil and religious liberties, and humanized the working classes last century." On the other hand, he criticized the young Cambridge Communists for the other side of the Reformation/Great Rebellion coin: they were puritans. Keynes's lifelong antipuritanism emerged in the question, Are Cambridge undergraduates disillusioned when they go to Russia, when they "find it dreadfully uncomfortable? Of course not. That is what they are looking for" (Hession 1984, p. 265).

Keynes firmly rejected communism after his own visit to Russia in 1925. He did not like the mass terror and extermination, caused partly by the speed of the revolutionary transformation and partly too, Keynes opined, by "some beastliness in the Russian nature—or in the Russian and Jewish natures when, as now, they are allied together." He also had strong doubts that

"Russian communism" would be able to "make Jews less avaricious" (Keynes 1925, pp. 37, 15).

Indeed, Keynes had long been anti-Semitic.[12] At Eton, Maynard wrote an essay titled "The Differences Between East and West," in which he condemned the Jews as an Eastern people who, because of "deep-rooted instincts that are antagonistic and therefore repulsive to the European," can no more be assimilated to European civilization than cats can be forced to love dogs (Skidelsky, 1986, p. 92). Later, as a British official at the Paris peace conference, Keynes wrote of his great admiration of Lloyd George's brutal anti-Semitic attack on the French Finance Minister, Louis-Lucien Klotz, who had tried to squeeze the defeated Germans for more gold in exchange for relieving the Allied food blockade.

First, there was Keynes's description of Klotz: "A short, plump, heavy-moustached Jew, well groomed, well kept, but with an unsteady, roving eye, and his shoulders a little bent with instinctive deprecation." Keynes then described the dramatic moment:

> Lloyd George had always hated him and despised him; and now saw in a twinkling that he could kill him. Women and children were starving, he cried, and here was M. Klotz prating and prating of his "goold." He leant forward and with a gesture of his hands indicated to everyone the image of a hideous Jew clutching a money bag. His eyes flashed and the words came out with a contempt so violent that he seemed almost to be spitting at him. The anti-Semitism, not far below the surface in such an assemblage as that one, was up in the heart of everyone. Everyone looked at Klotz with a momentary contempt and hatred; the poor man was bent over his seat, visibly cowering. We hardly knew what Lloyd George was saying, but the words "goold" and Klotz were repeated, and each time with exaggerated contempt.

---

[12] Earlier, Keynes had called for a "transformation of society," which "may require a reduction in the rate of interest toward the vanishing point within the next thirty years" (Keynes 1933, pp. 762).

At that point, Lloyd George came to the climax of his performance: turning to the French premier, Clemenceau, he warned that unless the French ceased their obstructive tactics against feeding the defeated Germans, three names would go down in history as the architects of Bolshevism in Europe: Lenin and Trotsky and ... as Keynes wrote, "The Prime Minister ceased. All around the room you could see each one grinning and whispering to his neighbor, 'Klotsky'" (Keynes 1949, p. 229; Skidelsky 1986, pp. 360, 362).

The point is that Keynes, who had never particularly liked Lloyd George before, was won over by his display of George's savage anti-Semitic pyrotechnics. "He can be amazing when one agrees with him," declared Keynes. "Never have I more admired his extraordinary powers" (1949, p. 225).[13]

But the major reason for Keynes's rejection of communism was simply that he could scarcely identify with the grubby proletariat. As Keynes wrote after his trip to Soviet Russia: "How can I adopt such a creed which, preferring the mud to the fish, exalts the boorish proletariat above the bourgeoisie and the intelligentsia who ... are the quality in life and surely carry the seeds of all human advancement?" (Hession 1984, p. 224).

Rejecting the proletarian socialism of the British Labour Party, Keynes made a stark and similar point: "It is a class war and the class is not my class. ... The class war would find me on the side of the educated bourgeoisie" (Brunner 1987, p. 28). John Maynard Keynes was a lifelong member of the British aristocracy, and he was not about to forget it.

---

[13] Keynes could rise above his generally anti-Semitic attitude, especially when a wealthy international banker, capable of conferring favors, was involved. Thus, we have seen that Edwin Samuel Montagu was Keynes's earliest and most important political patron; and Keynes also became fond of Germany's representative at the Paris peace conference, Dr. Carl Melchior: "In a sort of way I was in love with him" (Keynes 1949, p. 222). The fact that Melchior was a partner in the prominent international banking firm of M.M. Warburg and Company might have had something to do with Keynes's benign attitude.

Summing Up

WAS KEYNES, as Hayek maintained, a "brilliant scholar"? "Scholar" hardly, since Keynes was abysmally read in the economics literature: he was more of a buccaneer, taking a little bit of knowledge and using it to inflict his personality and fallacious ideas upon the world, with a drive continually fueled by an arrogance bordering on egomania. But Keynes had the good fortune to be born within the British elite, to be educated within the top economics circles (Eton/Cambridge/Apostles), and to be specially chosen by the powerful Alfred Marshall.

"Brilliant" is scarcely an apt word either. Clearly, Keynes was bright enough, but his most significant qualities were his arrogance, his unlimited self-confidence, and his avid will to power, to domination, to cutting a great swath through the arts, the social sciences, and the world of politics.

Furthermore, Keynes was scarcely a "revolutionary" in any real sense. He possessed the tactical wit to dress up ancient statist and inflationist fallacies with modern, pseudoscientific jargon, making them appear to be the latest findings of economic science. Keynes was thereby able to ride the tidal wave of statism and socialism, of managed and planning economies. Keynes eliminated economic theory's ancient role as spoilsport for inflationist and statist schemes, leading a new generation of economists on to academic power and to political pelf and privilege.

A more fitting term for Keynes would be "charismatic"—not in the sense of commanding the allegiance of millions but in being able to con and seduce important people—from patrons to politicians to students and even to opposing economists. A man who thought and acted in terms of power and brutal domination, who reviled the concept of moral principle, who was an eternal and sworn enemy of the bourgeoisie, of creditors, and of the thrifty middle class, who was a systematic liar, twisting truth to fit his own plan, who was a Fascist and an anti-Semite, Keynes was nevertheless able to cajole opponents and competitors.

Even as he cunningly turned his students against his colleagues, he was still able to cozen those same colleagues into intellectual surrender. Harassing and hammering away unfairly at Pigou, Keynes was yet able, at last and from beyond the grave, to wring an abject recantation from his old colleague. Similarly, he inspired his old foe Lionel Robbins to muse absurdly in his diary about the golden halo around Keynes's "godlike" head. He was able to convert to Keynesianism several Hayekians and Misesians who should have known—and undoubtedly did know—better: in addition to Abba Lerner, John Hicks, Kenneth Boulding, Nicholas Kaldor, and G.L.S. Shackle in England, there were also Fritz Machlup and Gottfried Haberler from Vienna, who landed at Johns Hopkins and Harvard, respectively.

Of all the Misesians of the early 1930s, the only economist completely uninfected by the Keynesian doctrine and personality was Mises himself. And Mises, in Geneva and then for years in New York without a teaching position, was removed from the influential academic scene. Even though Hayek remained anti-Keynesian, he too was touched by the Keynesian charisma. Despite everything, Hayek was proud to call Keynes a friend and indeed promoted the legend that Keynes, at the end of his life, was about to convert from his own Keynesianism.

Hayek's evidence for Keynes's alleged last-minute conversion is remarkably slight—based on two events in the final years of Keynes's life. First, in June 1944, upon reading *The Road to Serfdom*, Keynes, now at the pinnacle of his career as a wartime government planner, wrote a note to Hayek, calling it "a great book … morally and philosophically I find myself in agreement with virtually the whole of it." But why should this be interpreted as anything more than a polite note to a casual friend on the occasion of his first popular book?

Moreover, Keynes made it clear that, despite his amiable words, he never accepted the essential "slippery slope" thesis of Hayek, namely, that statism and central planning lead straight to totalitarianism. On the contrary, Keynes wrote that "moderate planning will be safe if those carrying it out are rightly oriented in their minds and hearts to the moral issue." This sentence, of course, rings true, for Keynes always believed that the installation of good men, namely, himself and the technicians and statesmen of his social class, was the only safeguard needed to check the powers of the rulers (Wilson 1982, pp. 64ff.).

Hayek proffers one other bit of flimsy evidence for Keynes's alleged recantation, which occurred during his final meeting with Keynes in 1946, the last year of Keynes's life. Hayek reports,

> A turn in the conversation made me ask him whether or not he was concerned about what some of his disciples were making of his theories. After a not very complimentary remark about the persons concerned he proceeded to reassure me: those ideas had been badly needed at the time he had launched them. But I need not be alarmed: if they should ever become dangerous I could rely upon him that he would again quickly swing round public opinion—indicating by a quick movement of his hand how rapidly that would be done. But three months later he was dead. (Hayek 1967, p. 348)[14]

Yet this was hardly a Keynes on the verge of recantation. Rather, this was vintage Keynes, a man who always held his sovereign ego

---

[14] Harry Johnson recorded a similar impression, at Keynes's presentation of his posthumously published paper on the balance of payments, in which Johnson concludes that Keynes's reference to "how much modernist stuff, gone wrong and turned sour and silly, is circulating in our system," refers to the left-Keynesian, or Marxo-Keynesian, Joan Robinson (Johnson 1978, pp. 159n).

higher than any principles, higher than any mere ideas, a man who relished the power he held. He could and would turn the world, set it right with a snap of his fingers, as he presumed to have done in the past.

Moreover, this statement was also vintage Keynes in terms of his long-held view of how to act properly when in or out of power. In the 1930s, prominent but out of power, he could speak and act "a little wild"; but now that he enjoyed the high seat of power, it was time to tone down the "poetic license." Joan Robinson and the other Marxo-Keynesians were making the mistake, from Keynes's point of view, of not subordinating their cherished ideas to the requirements of his prodigious position of power.

And so Hayek too, while never succumbing to Keynes's ideas, did fall under his charismatic spell. In addition to creating the legend of Keynes's change of heart, why did Hayek not demolish *The General Theory* as he had Keynes's *Treatise on Money?* Hayek admitted to a strategic error, that he had not bothered to do so because Keynes was notorious for changing his mind, so Hayek did not think then that *The General Theory* would last. Moreover, as Mark Skousen has noted in chapter 1 of this volume, Hayek apparently pulled his punches in the 1940s in order to avoid interfering with Britain's Keynesian financing of the war effort—certainly an unfortunate example of truth suffering at the hands of presumed political expediency

Later economists continued to hew a revisionist line, maintaining absurdly that Keynes was merely a benign pioneer of uncertainty theory (Shackle and Lachmann), or that he was a prophet of the idea that search costs were highly important in the labor market (Clower and Leijonhufvud). None of this is true. That Keynes was a Keynesian—of that much derided Keynesian system provided by Hicks, Hansen, Samuelson, and Modigliani—is the only explanation that makes any sense of Keynesian economics.

Yet Keynes was much more than a Keynesian. Above all, he was the extraordinarily pernicious and malignant figure that we have examined in this chapter: a charming but power-driven statist Machiavelli, who embodied some of the most malevolent trends and institutions of the 20th century.

Bibliography

Brunner, Karl. 1987. "The Sociopolitical Vision of Keynes," in David A. Reese, ed., *The Legacy of Keynes*. San Francisco: Harper and Row.

Corry, Bernard. 1978. "Keynes in the History of Economic Thought," in A. Thirlwall, ed., *Keynes and Laissez Faire*. London: Macmillan.

Corry, Bernard. 1986. "Keynes's Economics: A Revolution in Economic Theory or Economic Policy?" in R.D. Collison Black, ed., *Ideas in Economics*. Totowa, N.J.: Barnes and Noble.

Crabtree, Derek. 1980. "Cambridge Intellectual Currents of 1900," in Crabtree and Thirlwall 1980.

Crabtree, Derek, and A.P. Thirlwall, eds. 1980. *Keynes and the Bloomsbury Group*. London: Macmillan.

Cross, Colin. 1963. *The Fascists in Britain*. New York: St. Martin's Press.

Deacon, Richard. 1986. *The Cambridge Apostles*. New York: Farrar, Straus and Giroux.

Gillies, D.A. 1973. *An Objective Theory of Probability*. London: Methuen.

Harris, Seymour, ed. 1948. *The New Economics*. New York: Alfred A. Knopf.

Harrod, Roy. 1951. *The Life of John Maynard Keynes*. London: Macmillan.

Harrod, Roy. 1957. "Review of Clive Bell's Old Friends." *Economic Journal.*

Hayek, Friedrich A. 1931a. "Reflections on the Pure Theory of Money of Mr. J. M. Keynes." *Economica* 11.

______.1931b. "A Rejoinder to Mr. Keynes." *Economica* 11.

______.1932. "Reflections on the Pure Theory of Money of Mr. J.M. Keynes (continued)." *Economica* 12.

______.1944. *The Road to Serfdom*. Chicago: University of Chicago Press.

______.1967. *Studies in Philosophy, Politics and Economics*. Chicago: University of Chicago Press.

______.1984 [1956]. "Tribute to Ludwig von Mises," in Margit von Mises, *My Life with Ludwig von Mises*. 2d ed. Cedar Falls, Iowa: Center for Futures Education.

Hazlitt, Henry. 1973 [1959]. *The Failure of the "New Economics."* 2d ed. New Rochelle, N.Y.: Arlington House.

Hession, Charles H. 1984. *John Maynard Keynes*. New York: Macmillan.

Hodge, Ian. 1986. *Baptized Inflation*. Tyler, Tex.: Institute for Christian Economics.

Holroyd, Michael. 1967. *Lytton Strachey: A Critical Biography.* 2 vols. London: Heinemann.

Hutt, William H. 1974. *A Rehabilitation of Say's Law*. Columbus: Ohio State University Press.

Johnson, Elizabeth, and Harry G. Johnson. 1978. *The Shadow of Keynes*. Oxford: Basil Blackwell.

Keynes, John Maynard. 1914. "Review of Mises." *Economic Journal* 24.

______.1921. *A Treatise on Probability*. London: Macmillan.

______.1925. *A Short View of Russia*. London: Hogarth Press.

______.1930a. *A Treatise on Money.* 2 vols. London: Macmillan.

______.1930b. "Sir Oswald Mosley's Manifesto." *Nation and Atheneum* (13 December).

______.1933. "National Self-Sufficiency." *Yale Review* 22.

______.1936. *The General Theory of Employment, Interest and Money.* London: Macmillan.

______.1949. *Essays and Sketches in Biography.* New York: Meridian Books.

______.1971. *Activities, 1906–1914: India and Cambridge. The Collected Writings of John Maynard Keynes.* Vol. XV. London: Macmillan.

______.1972 [1951]. *Essays in Biography. The Collected Writings of John Maynard Keynes.* Vol. X. London: Macmillan.

______.1973 [1936]. *The General Theory of Employment, Interest and Money. The Collected Writings of John Maynard Keynes.* Vol. VII. London.

Keynes, John Neville. 1955 [1891]. *The Scope and Method of Political Economy.* New York: Kelley and Millman.

Mises, Ludwig von. 1966. [1949]. *Human Action: A Treatise on Economics.* 3d ed. Chicago: Henry Regnery.

Mises, Richard von. 1951. *Probability, Statistics and Truth.* 2d ed. London: Allen and Unwin.

Moggridge, D.E. 1969. *The Return to Gold, 1925: The Formation of Economic Policy and Its Critics.* Cambridge: Cambridge University Press.

Moore, G.E. 1903. *Principia Ethica.* Cambridge: Cambridge University Press.

Mosley, Sir Oswald. 1968. *My Life.* New Rochelle, N.Y.: Arlington House.

O'Brien, D.P. 1988. *Lionel Robbins.* New York: St. Martin's Press.

Parrini, Carl P., and Martin J. Sklar. 1983. "New Thinking about the Market, 1896–1904: Some American Economists on Investment and the Theory of Surplus Capital." *Journal of Economic History* 43.

Perlman, Morris. 1989. "Adam Smith and the Paternity of the Real Bills Doctrine." *History of Political Economy* 21.

Pigou, A.C. 1933. *The Theory of Unemployment.* London: Macmillan.

______.1950. *Keynes's General Theory: A Retrospective View*. London: Macmillan.

Robbins, Lionel. 1934. *The Great Depression*. London: Macmillan.

______.1971. *Autobiography of an Economist.* London: Macmillan.

Rosenberg, Emily S. 1985. "Foundations of United States International Financial Power: Gold Standard Diplomacy, 1900–1905." *Business History Review* 59.

Rothbard, Murray N. 1970 [1962]. *Man, Economy, and State*. Los Angeles: Nash Publishing.

______. 1988. *Ludwig von Mises: Scholar, Creator, Hero.* Auburn, Ala.: Mises Institute.

Rutten, Andrew. 1989. "Mr. Keynes on the Classics: A Suggestive Misinterpretation?" Unpublished manuscript.

Samuelson, Paul A. 1948 [1946]. "Lord Keynes and the General Theory," in Harris 1948. Originally appeared in *Econometrica* (July 1946).

Skidelsky, Robert. 1975. *Oswald Mosley*. New York: Holt, Rinehart and Winston.

______.1983. *John Maynard Keynes: Hopes Betrayed, 1883–1920.* London: Macmillan.

______.1986. *John Maynard Keynes: Hopes Betrayed, 1883–1920.* New York: Viking.

Trescott, Paul B. 1987. "J.M. Keynes as a Marshallian: Comment." *Journal of Economic Issues* 21.

Welch, Colin. 1986. "Review of Skidelsky." *The American Spectator* (December).

Wilson, Tom. 1982. "Policy in War and Peace: The Recommendations of J.M. Keynes," in A.P. Thirlwall, ed., *Keynes as a Policy Adviser*. London: Macmillan.